10

PEOPLE
THAT CHANGED
THE WORLD

Written by Ben Hubbard

WAYLAND

www.waylandbooks.co.uk

First published in 2015 by Wayland
Copyright © Wayland, 2015

Editors: Julia Adams; Katie Woolley
Designer: Peter Clayman

Dewey number: 920'.02–dc23
ISBN 978 0 7502 9129 3
Library eBook ISBN 978 0 7502 9130 9

Printed in China

10 9 8 7 6 5 4 3 2 1

Picture acknowledgements: Cover: © Louise Gubb/Corbis SABA; p. 1, p. 3 (third from left), p. 21, back cover (bottom right): © Bettmann/Corbis; p. 2 (far left), p. 6, p. 28, back cover (top left): © Sandro Vannini/Corbis; p. 2 (2nd from left), p. 9: © Leemage/Corbis; p. 2 (3rd from left), p. 4, p. 11: © Stefano Bianchetti/Corbis; p. 2 (4th from left), p. 13: © Underwood & Underwood/Corbis; p. 2 (5th from left), p. 5 (left), p. 15: © Hulton-Deutsch Collection/Corbis; p.3 (far left), p. 17: © Bettmann/Corbis; p. 3 (2nd from left left), p. 19: © Heritage images/Corbis; p. 3 (4th from left), p. 23: © Sygma/Corbis; p. 3 (5th from left), p. 5, p. 25: © Sasa Kralj/ZUMA Press/Corbis; p. 7: © Leemage/Corbis; p. 8: © Wayland images; p. 10: © Tarker/Corbis; p. 12: © Corbis; p. 14: © Corbis; p. 16: © Guenter Schindler/dpa/Corbis; p. 18, p. 31: © Steven Vidler/Corbis; p. 20: © Bettmann/Corbis; p. 22: © Orjan F. Ellingvag/Dagbladet/Corbis; p. 24: © David Turnley/Corbis; p. 26 (top right): © Alfredo Dagli Orti/The Art Archive/Corbis; p. 26 (top left): © Stefano Bianchetti/Corbis; p. 26 (bottom right): © Hulton-Deutsch Collection/Corbis; p. 26 (bottom left): © Hulton-Deutsch Collection/Corbis; p. 27 (top left): © Yevgeny Khaldei/Agentur Voller Ernst/dpa/Corbis; p. 27 (centre): © Bettmann/Corbis; p. 27 (centre right): Science Source/Science Photo Library; p. 27 (centre left): © Andrew Brusso/Corbis; p. 27 (bottom left): © Kim Kulish/Corbis; p. 29 (top right): © The Print Collector/Corbis; p. 29 (centre): © Corbis; p. 29 (bottom left): © Robert Wallis/SIPA/Corbis; all images used as graphic elements: Shutterstock.

The website addresses (URLs) included in this book were valid at the time of going to press. However, it is possible that contents or addresses may change following the publication of this book. No responsibility for any such changes can be accepted by either the author or the Publisher.

Every attempt has been made to clear copyright. Should there be any inadvertent omission, please apply to the publisher for rectification.

Wayland, an imprint of Hachette Children's Group
Part of Hodder & Stoughton
Carmelite House
50 Victoria Embankment
London
EC4Y 0DZ

An Hachette UK Company
www.hachette.co.uk
www.hachettechildrens.co.uk

MIX
Paper from responsible sources
FSC
www.fsc.org
FSC® C104740

Contents

INTRODUCTION

Choosing ten people who changed the world is a tricky task. Many more than just ten individuals have influenced the course of human history. However, only a few people are remembered today. In modern times, the most famous people in the world are often celebrities, sports stars or global leaders. But will they still be talked about in 100, or even 1000 years? To change the world, a person has to do something so extraordinary that it creates a legacy lasting far beyond their own death.

Astronomer Galileo Galilei is often called the 'Father of Modern Science.'

The ten people featured in this book came from different places and different times, and each one had a unique and enormous impact on the world that is still felt today. Some voyaged to undiscovered lands in the name of exploration or conquest. Others explored the world of science, to help humans on earth or explain the entire universe. Many tried to make people's lives better, while others sought to destroy whole cultures and civilisations. Some found that the smallest action could have a huge impact on society. Others showed that you do not need to be rich or powerful to make a difference – ordinary people can change the world, too.

Many people suffered while trying to change the world. They had to fight prejudice, discrimination and ignorance in their own lifetimes. Some world-changers lived their whole lives without understanding the significance of their actions. Others died wishing their impact had been greater in their lifetime.

While there is no standard model for someone who changes the world, there is one thing that unites the people in this book. Despite their differences, they all wanted to transform things and create something new. It is for this reason that all ten figures, for better or worse, changed the world we live in.

Florence Nightingale was a war heroine who helped found modern nursing.

Civil rights leader Nelson Mandela was South Africa's first black

ALEXANDER THE GREAT

In 334 BCE, Alexander the Great led 35,000 soldiers into Asia Minor (now part of Turkey) and began a ten-year campaign of conquest and control. With the 5-metre long 'sarissa' spear at the heart of his army, Alexander invaded a massive area of Persian territory stretching from modern-day Turkey to Iraq. It was the largest empire the ancient world had ever known. Alexander had vowed to crush the Greeks' oldest enemy, the Persians, since he was a boy. But Alexander himself was not Greek: he was Macedonian. During Alexander's childhood, Macedonia was a small kingdom that lay next to the great civilisation of Greece. The Greeks considered the Macedonians to be uncivilised barbarians. But Alexander's father, Philip II of Macedon, did something no Greek could achieve – he united all of Greece under his rule.

Alexander had been brought up in the Greek traditions and educated by the Greek philosopher Aristotle. He even modelled himself on the heroes of Greek myth and legend, Achilles and Hercules. So when his father was assassinated in 336 BCE, the newly crowned Alexander decided to conquer Persia. Alexander's army did not lose a single battle as it destroyed all Persian opposition. In 331 BCE, Alexander crushed the army of Persian King Darius III at the Battle of Gaugamela, and was proclaimed King of Asia. Alexander, however, yearned for new conquests. He marched his men through modern-day Afghanistan and Pakistan, but they would not follow him into India. Reluctantly, Alexander turned back. Alexander had conquered over two million square miles of land. Instead of dying a hero's death in battle, he died from a fever, possibly caused by a mosquito bite.

This ancient bust reveals Alexander's face to the modern world.

339 BCE: MACEDONIAN KING PHILIP UNITES GREECE UNDER HIS RULE .....

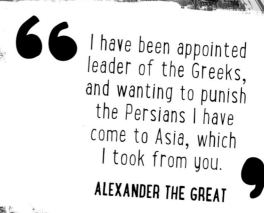

> **66** I have been appointed leader of the Greeks, and wanting to punish the Persians I have come to Asia, which I took from you. **99**
>
> **ALEXANDER THE GREAT**

A painting of Alexander's victory over the Persians at the 333 BCE Battle of Issus.

Changing the world

Alexander's life was short, but he left a lasting legacy. In the former Persian Empire, he founded 70 new cities, created trade between the East and the West and spread the ideas of ancient Greece throughout his conquered lands. Today, this Greek influence can still be seen among the ruins of cities such as Alexandria in Egypt. Alexander allowed local customs to live alongside Greek culture.

helping his conquered subjects adapt to their new ruler. Yet, building a lasting civilisation proved beyond the King of Macedonia. After his death, Alexander's empire crumbled. Later, his accomplishments would serve as inspiration for many future warlords. Julius Caesar, Napoleon and Hitler all tried to copy Alexander's conquests, but none of them was able to match up to the man himself.

CHRISTOPHER COLUMBUS

Ten weeks after setting sail from Spain, Christopher Columbus reached the sandy shores of a new land. He assumed he was somewhere in Asia, known then as the 'Indies', and called the native inhabitants 'Indians'. But Columbus was nowhere near Asia. Instead, he had accidently reached the islands today called the Bahamas, in the Caribbean. Over the next 12 years, Columbus made three return voyages to various islands of the Caribbean, as well as central America and Venezuela, on behalf of the Spanish crown. Columbus was one of the first Europeans to visit these places and he later became known as 'the man who discovered America'.

Columbus was born in the Italian city of Genoa and brought up during the Age of Discovery when Europeans were searching for new sea routes to Asia in their hunt for trade, wealth and land. Wishing to join these explorers, Columbus persuaded Queen Isabella and King Ferdinand of Spain to finance a voyage to Asia. Most European captains sailed around Africa to Asia, but Columbus attempted to reach it by crossing the Atlantic Ocean.

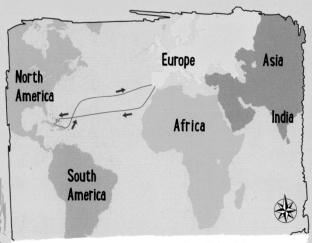

Columbus' route across the Atlantic Ocean to the Americas and back.

In 1492, Columbus set out with the fleet of ships that would carry him to the Americas: the Santa Maria, the Pinta and the Niña. Columbus claimed every territory he visited for Spain and was made 'Admiral of the Seven Seas' and 'Viceroy of the Indies'. However, reports reached the Spanish court of Columbus' brutal treatment of the native inhabitants and he was removed from his position as viceroy. Columbus and his heirs tried to sue the Spanish court for money made from his discovered territories, but were unsuccessful. He died a disappointed man in 1506.

STATS PANEL

Lived: 1451–1506

World-changing moments:
Discovered the Americas.

Titles: Admiral of the Seven Seas
and Viceroy of the Indies.

Fact: Columbus convinced the Spanish court
of the riches to be found in the new world
by bringing back gifts of gold, spices,
parrots and human captives.

Christopher Columbus
is shown landing in the
Bahamas for the first time.

Changing the world

Although the Vikings had visited the Americas several centuries earlier, Columbus was the first explorer to open up the continents to Europe. This meant an exchange between the two worlds of cultures, people, plants, animals and diseases. This world-changing moment had some devastating consequences for the native peoples of the Americas. The Taino Indians of Hispaniola suffered enslavement and brutality at the hands of Columbus, while others were wiped out by European smallpox. These devastating developments continued in the centuries to come as European nations conquered more of the Americas, with the Aztecs, Incas and Native Americans all suffering similar fates. Columbus himself would never have dreamed of this legacy. He went to the grave still believing the lands he had discovered were in Asia.

GALILEO GALILEI

Galileo Galilei was an Italian astronomer who was imprisoned for his revolutionary ideas about the solar system. Educated as a mathematician, Galileo's life took a dramatic turn in 1609 when he heard about the invention of the telescope. He set about building a superior model so he could observe the stars above. Soon afterwards, Galileo discovered four moons travelling around Jupiter. This lead him to believe that the planets were also travelling around a large body – the sun. The theory that the sun, and not the earth, was at the centre of the universe had already been put forward by Polish astronomer Nicholas Copernicus. But this view, now also supported by Galileo, contradicted the teachings of the Catholic Church. The Church accused Galileo of heresy – a serious crime that could result in a death sentence.

Galileo Galilei explains his theory about the Earth's place in the universe.

Galileo was a gentleman of the court in Florence, Italy, and managed to escape punishment for supporting Copernicus' theory. However, in 1616, the Church forbade Galileo from speaking out about it. For years he remained silent, but the theory emerged once more in Galileo's book *Dialogue on the Two Chief World Systems* in 1632. Galileo was put on trial by the Roman Catholic Church and found guilty of heresy. He was sentenced to life imprisonment, which he spent under house arrest in a villa in Arcetri, near Florence. From here, Galileo continued his investigations into physics and astronomy, and made new discoveries in both areas. In his later life, Galileo suffered from various illnesses and he was completely blind at the time of his death.

1609: GALILEO OBSERVES THE SKY THROUGH HIS CUSTOM-MADE TELESCOPE

Galileo observes the sky through his custom-made telescope.

Changing the world

Galileo's contributions revolutionised the world of science and religion. As an astronomer, Galileo made a series of important discoveries with his telescope: he found that the moon is rough not smooth, and that there were many more stars in the Milky Way than previously believed. Galileo was interested in other scientific fields, too, and his work later contributed to Isaac Newton's Laws of Motion.

He also helped develop the 'scientific method', the process used in scientific investigation. However, it is for his conflict with the Church that Galileo is best remembered. He refused to accept the Church's ideas unless they could be scientifically proven. He began the separation of religious belief and scientific thought. It is also one of the reasons Galileo is known today as the 'Father of Modern Science'.

MARIE CURIE

Marie Curie was a world-changing scientist who had to fight to be educated and work in a field dominated by men. Curie was born Marie Sklodowska in Poland at a time when women were banned from higher education. To escape this policy, Curie attended a secret University in Warsaw before moving to the Sorbonne University in Paris, France. Curie had little knowledge of French and barely any money. She lived in a small attic room where she had to wear several layers of clothing to keep warm. Curie often could not afford to buy food and sometimes fainted from hunger. She also faced discrimination at the university for being a woman. Curie did not give up despite these obstacles and obtained degrees in both maths and physics.

STATS PANEL

Lived: 1867-1934

World-changing moments: Discovered the chemical elements radium and polonium.

Awards: The Nobel Prize for Physics and the Nobel Prize for Chemistry.

Fact: Curie was the first women to win a Nobel Prize, the only woman to win the Prize in two fields, and the only person to win in multiple sciences.

> Nothing in life is to be feared, it is only to be understood. Now is the time to understand more, so that we may fear less.
>
> Marie Curie

Marie helped change attitudes towards female scientists.

It was at university that Marie met and married physicist Pierre Curie. Together, the pair discovered the chemical elements radium and polonium and coined the term 'radioactivity'. This won the Curies the Nobel Prize for Physics in 1903. It was the first time a woman had been awarded the prize. But tragedy struck when Pierre was knocked down and killed by a horse-drawn carriage. Left to bring up their two daughters alone, Curie continued her work and was made professor at the University of Paris in her husband's place. Curie went on to isolate the element pure radium, a groundbreaking achievement which won her the Nobel Prize for Chemistry in 1911. Her research would lead to the use of radiotherapy in medicine, but it was also took its toll on Curie's health. In 1934 she died from leukaemia, caused by her long-term exposure to radiation.

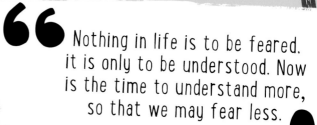

1903: CURIE WINS THE NOBEL PRIZE AND COINS THE PHRASE 'RADIOACTIVITY'.....

Marie worked side by side with her husband, Pierre, until his death.

Changing the world

Marie Curie changed the world through her scientific discoveries and by changing attitudes towards female scientists. Her research into radioactivity provided a major scientific breakthrough that led to the use of radiation therapy to fight cancer and helped later scientists better understand the atom. It also enabled Curie to develop an X-ray service for war-time doctors who used it to locate shrapnel and broken bones in patients before surgery.

Curie even drove the vans containing portable X-ray units to hospitals on the frontline during the First World War (1914–1918). Despite her accomplishments, Curie had to fight for her career – first to be educated and then to prove her worth as a scientist. It was through her extraordinary academic ability that Curie was able to transform attitudes towards women in the scientific community, and help secure their place within it as equal partners.

FLORENCE NIGHTINGALE

Florence Nightingale was born into a wealthy family during the Industrial Revolution and lived a privileged life. While many English people struggled to survive working in factories and coal mines, Nightingale's time was spent socialising, entertaining and taking holidays. However, she became deeply unsatisfied. Her ambition was to become a nurse, but her parents were against the idea. Nurses at that time were untrained and were considered little more than servants by the upper classes. But Nightingale went against her parents' wishes and became a nurse despite their objections. At 33 years old, her first job was running a private hospital in London. She would go on to found the profession of modern nursing and become a British war heroine.

A bird's-eye view of the British cavalry camp during the Crimean War.

Nightingale became famous after she led a team of nurses to tend to British soldiers during the Crimean War. She was horrified at the conditions in the army hospital in Scutari in modern-day Turkey. Wounded men lay unattended on the floor of filthy, overcrowded wards, infested with rats, fleas and lice. Nightingale transformed the hospital by introducing order, sanitation and patient care. She worked for twenty hours a day and tended to the soldiers late into the night, which earned her the title 'Lady with the Lamp'. Newspaper reports about Nightingale made her famous in Britain before she even returned home. Yet, Nightingale's own health suffered back in England and she spent the last 50 years of her life confined to her house. Despite this, she opened the Nightingale School for Nurses in London in 1860, the first of its kind in the world.

> **66** Were there none who were discontented with what they have, the world would never reach anything better. **99**
>
> **Florence Nightingale**

Florence Nightingale was an important figure in the struggle for equal rights for women.

Changing the world

Florence Nightingale changed the world of nursing and subsequently changed commonly held views about women in the workplace. From the moment Nightingale entered the nursing profession, it was her dream to train nurses. Nightingales school for nurses and her textbook *Notes on Nursing* set a benchmark for modern nursing. The Nightingale nurses quickly gained a reputation for the excellence that Nightingales name is still associated with today.

It is for this reason that Nightingale is considered to have laid the foundations for modern nursing. But Nightingale's work also marked an important moment for womens rights. Although she was expected to stay at home and raise a family, Nightingale showed that women were capable of taking up and succeeding in professional occupations that had previously been closed to them.

ADOLF HITLER

"The personification of the devil as the symbol of all evil assumes the living shape of the Jew."

These are Adolf Hitler's words from *Mein Kampf* (My Struggle), a memoir which outlined his hatred of Jewish people and his plans for a new world order. It was with these plans in mind that Hitler caused the outbreak of the Second World War in 1939 and the deaths of millions, including the extermination of six million Jews. When Hitler wrote *Mein Kampf* in 1925, he was an almost unknown figure. He was also in jail, having been imprisoned in 1923 for trying to lead an armed uprising against the German government. At that time, Hitler was the leader of the fascist National Socialist German Workers' Party, also known as the Nazi party. He had joined the Munich-based party after fighting as a soldier in the First World War.

One of Hitler's speeches rallying the German people to his cause.

The Auschwitz-Birkenau concentration camp where over 1 million people were executed.

After being released from prison, Hitler set about putting his plans into action. By 1933, the Nazi party was in government and Hitler was the country's leader. He immediately began strengthening Germany's military and introduced a series of anti-Jewish laws, which were enforced with violence. Hitler's invasion of Poland in 1939 started the Second World War. As his army conquered more countries across Europe, Jews and other people considered racially inferior were rounded up and killed. After two successful years of war, the tide turned agains Hitler. By April 1945, Allied troops had won back all of Europe's conquered territories and were attacking Berlin. On 30 April, Hitler committed suicide in his bunker.

1925: HITLER OUTLINES HIS HATRED OF JEWS IN HIS BOOK 'MEIN KAMPF'... 1945: THE WORLD

Changing the world

Hitler showed the power of one man in leading a nation to commit war and mass-murder on a world-changing scale. It is widely accepted that Hitler's beliefs led to the deaths of 29 million soldiers and civilians during the Second World War. However, the true extent of the war was not known until after the fighting had finished. Across German occupied territories, over 300 concentration camps had been created to execute people or work them to death. The mass extermination of Jews, Roma people, homosexuals, communists and anyone else Hitler's government considered its enemy, became known as the Holocaust. The total number of people executed by the Nazis is thought to be over 19 million. It is this unimaginable horror, alongside the destruction of much of Europe, that makes up Hitler's terrible legacy.

ALAN TURING

STATS PANEL

Lived: 1912-1954

World-changing moments: Cracked the Enigma code.

Titles: Called the Father of Computer Science.

Fact: Turing was a talented long-distance runner who would often run the 40 miles (64 kilometres) from Bletchley Park to London for top-secret wartime meetings.

Alan Turing was often described as an eccentric: he wore a gas mask in summer to prevent hay fever and chained his mug to a radiator at work so it would not be stolen. He was also a genius who helped the Allies win the Second World War by cracking the Nazi code-making machine, Enigma. Turing was hired to work at Bletchley Park, the British government's code-breaking headquarters, after studying mathematics at Cambridge University. At Bletchley Park, Turing developed the 'bombe', a device that could decipher Enigma's coded messages. The Nazis considered their Enigma code-making machine impossible to crack and it was used for all high-level operations by the German army, air force and navy. Cracking Enigma created a breakthrough moment in the war that enabled the Allies to unscramble German messages and ultimately defeat them in battle.

Alan Turing not only cracked the Nazi Enigma machine but also helped develop modern computing.

The Enigma code-making machine used by the Nazis.

After the war, Turing helped found modern computer science through his work at the National Physical Laboratory and Manchester University. Turing's ACE (Automatic Computing Engine) and the Manchester Mark 1 were among the first programmable computers ever invented. Turing also laid the groundwork for artificial intelligence and his 'Turing test' is still used today to tell whether an internet user is a computer or a real person. Despite his valuable work, Turing's world was turned upside down in 1952. This was the year he was arrested and found guilty of homosexuality, a punishable crime in Britain until 1967. Although he escaped going to jail, Turing's security clearance was revoked, meaning he could no longer work for the government. Driven to despair, Turing committed suicide in 1954.

1945: TURING AWARDED AN OBE FOR CRACKING ENIGMA ..... 1952: TURING PROSECUTED

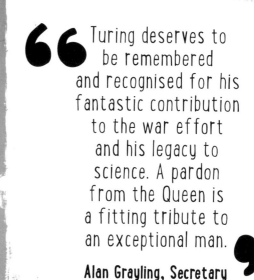

Changing the world

Turing's work cracking Enigma saved countless lives during the Second World War and was described by Prime Minister Winston Churchill as "The single biggest contribution to Allied victory in the war against Nazi Germany." It was for his world-changing wartime work that Turing was awarded an OBE (Order of the British Empire). It is a mark of his genius that Turing is also remembered for his contributions to modern computing. Turing has often been called "The Father of Computer Science" and his name is still celebrated through awards. computer programmes. stamps and plaques. Despite his world-changing contributions. Turing's life was cut short in the most tragic of circumstances. In 2009. the British Government apologised for the "appalling" way Turing had been treated for being homosexual and in 2013 the Queen granted him a posthumous pardon.

ROSA PARKS

On an ordinary December day in 1955, 42-year-old seamstress Rosa Parks boarded the bus to get home. Parks was an ordinary working woman who was unknown to the world – but she was about to change history. Parks sat down as usual on the bus in the seats reserved for black people. In Montgomery, Alabama, USA at that time, buses were segregated into a white section at the front and a black section at the back. But as the bus filled up, the driver asked Parks to stand so a white man could take her seat. She replied that she would not. The driver called the police and Parks was arrested and later fined by the courts. In the 1950s, Alabama was one of several southern American states that had segregated public spaces. This meant black people were banned from using the same facilities as white people, including park benches, cafés, toilets and libraries.

Rosa Parks' small protest helped ignite the American civil rights movement.

Rosa Parks sits by a white man after the government rules segregation on buses is illegal.

News of Parks' protest on the bus sparked a 381-day boycott of Montgomery buses by black people. The boycott was organised by a young minister called Martin Luther King Jr., who went on to become a famous leader of the American civil rights movement. The boycott worked. In 1956, the U.S. Supreme Court ruled that the segregation law was unconstitutional and the black section on Montgomery buses was abolished. The ruling was a great victory in the fight for equal rights for black people that sparked non-violent protests across America. Parks, however, was fired from her job as a result of her protest. She later worked as a secretary for a congressman and co-founded the Rosa and Raymond Parks Institute for Self Development, which provided career training for young people.

1955: ROSA PARKS REFUSES TO STAND FOR A WHITE MAN ON A SEGREGATED BUS .....

> 66 I don't know why I wasn't, but I didn't feel afraid. I had decided that I would have to know once and for all what rights I had as a human being and a citizen, even in Montgomery, Alabama. 99
>
> **Rosa Parks (1956)**

Changing the world

To the eyes of the world, Rosa Parks was an ordinary woman living an ordinary life before that fateful day in 1955. But through her quiet, courageous action she changed the course of history. In the 1950s, many black people in the American South began to fight the policy of segregation. When Parks was a girl, she watched the schoolbus for white children only drive past as she walked the several miles to school. It was because of

Parks' protest on the bus years later and the civil rights protests which followed, that black people achieved legal equality in the 1960s. This gave them the same rights to vote, live, be educated and sit in the same places as white people. It is for this reason, Rosa Parks, who seemed like an unremarkable seamstress from Montgomery, is today remembered as the 'Mother of the Civil Rights Movement'.

2013: FIRST BLACK US PRESIDENT BARACK OBAMA SITS ON THE ROSA PARKS BUS EXHIBIT

OSAMA BIN LADEN

Osama bin Laden was the leader of Islamist terror group al-Qaeda and the mastermind behind the terror attacks on 11 September 2001 in New York, USA. Bin Laden was one of 50 children born to self-made billionaire Muhammad bin Laden and was brought up in Saudi Arabia. At university, bin Laden developed radical Islamist ideas and a strong hatred of Western governments. In 1979, he travelled to Afghanistan to gain military training and help the local Taliban fight against the Soviet Union's occupation of the country. The Taliban is a group of Islamic fundamentalists made up of Afghanistani tribal warriors. Bin Laden raised funds for the Taliban and also created a military network of Arab fighters that would later become al-Qaeda. Al-Qaeda became known for its tactics of suicide attacks and the bombing of buildings.

STATS PANEL

Lived: 1957-2011

World-changing moments: Masterminded the 9/11 terror attacks on the USA.

Fact: From 2001-2011 bin Laden was at the top of the USA's most wanted list, with a US$25 million bounty on his head.

Osama Bin Laden, the mastermind behind the 9/11 attacks on the USA.

One of the World Trade Center towers after a plane has been flown into it.

In the 1990s, al-Qaeda began a series of terrorist attacks against the USA that included the bombing of its embassies in Kenya and Nairobi. In 1998, bin Laden called for all Muslims to kill Americans and their allies wherever they could. This led to al-Qaeda hijacking four planes for its 9/11 attacks. The attacks resulted in the destruction of New York's two World Trade Center skyscrapers and the deaths of nearly 3,000 people. In response, the United States ordered the military overthrow of the Taliban in Afghanistan. In 2011, bin Laden was found hiding in a walled compound in the city of Abbottabad, Pakistan. He was killed during a US raid on the compound and his body buried at sea.

2001: OSAMA BIN LADEN LAUNCHES HIS 9/11 ATTACKS ON AMERICA .....

Changing the world

Osama bin Laden's terrorist actions have had a massive impact on modern civilisation. The main objective of bin Laden's al-Qaeda was to end the presence of the USA and other Western countries in Muslim countries. But instead, the 9/11 attacks led the USA and other Western countries to begin to fight a global war on terror that continues today. Western attacks within Muslim territories has led to the deaths of thousands of military personnel and civilians alike. Everyday lives have also been affected, as fears of further terrorist attacks and heightened security in public places have become regular features of modern life in Western cities. The war continues against al-Qaeda and other terror groups that include the Islamic State of Iraq and Syria (ISIS). As the world still grapples with the issues caused by bin Laden and al-Qaeda, it is difficult to predict how severe and long-lasting his legacy will be.

NELSON MANDELA

In 1964, Nelson Mandela was found guilty of treason and narrowly escaped the death penalty. Instead, the South African civil rights leader was sentenced to 27 years in prison. The government thought Mandela's imprisonment would signal the end of his fight against its policy of apartheid. Apartheid was South Africa's segregation of races, which banned black people from voting, forced them to live in special 'black' areas with poor conditions. However, the government was wrong to think it could silence Mandela. Instead, his imprisonment brought Mandela attention and support from around the world and put pressure on South Africa's government to abandon apartheid.

STATS PANEL

Lived: 1918-2013

Awards: Mandela won more than 250 awards during his lifetime, including the 1993 Nobel Peace Prize.

Titles: President to South Africa 1994-99 and called the 'Founding Father of Democracy.'

Fact: Mandela was a member of the tribal Xhosa-speaking Tembu people and was often called by his clan name, Madiba.

Nelson Mandela leaves prison for the first time after 27 years.

Rolihlahla 'Nelson' Mandela first began his struggle against oppression as a law student in Johannesburg. Here, he joined the African National Congress (ANC), a party that fought for the rights of black people. Apartheid was introduced in 1948 and the ANC battled against the racist policy through non-violent protests. Following the shootings of 69 anti-apartheid protestors during a demonstration in the black township of Sharpeville in 1960, the government declared a state of emergency and banned the ANC. In response, the ANC abandoned its policy of non-violence and Mandela sought out military support for the party in other countries. When he returned, Mandela was arrested and imprisoned. Twenty-seven years later, the South African government bowed to international pressure by releasing Mandela. Mandela then worked with the government to abolish apartheid in South Africa. He became the country's first black president in 1993 and died a free man twenty years later.

1964: NELSON MANDELA IS BRANDED A TERRORIST AND IMPRISONED FOR 27 YEARS

Nelson Mandela used his fame to promote important causes until his death.

Changing the world

At the time of his death, Nelson Mandela was one of the most famous figures in the world. In South Africa, he was known simply as the 'Founding Father of Democracy'. For those living under apartheid, Mandela was their liberator and champion. Mandela's imprisonment did little to stop his influence and instead brought widespread international condemnation. After his release in 1993, Mandela inspired the world by working with the government that had imprisoned him to create a new South Africa with equal rights for all. His work with then president F. W. de Klerk to achieve this aim made both men co-winners of the 1993 Nobel Peace Prize. After standing down as president, Mandela continued to use his fame to promote good causes, including raising awareness of the deadly AIDS/HIV virus. Today, Mandela's image is instantly recognisable as a symbol for the fight against oppression and a reminder that people have the ability to change the course of human history for the better.

10 OTHER PEOPLE THAT CHANGED THE WORLD

1. Leonardo da Vinci (1452-1519)

An artist, engineer, scientist and inventor who was considered one of the most creative minds of the Italian Renaissance. Painter of the famous *Mona Lisa*, da Vinci also drew up plans for a bicycle and helicopter 500 years before they were invented.

2. William Shakespeare (1564-1616)

An English writer, poet and actor considered by many to be the greatest playwright of all time. His work may be over 400 years old, but it is still taught in schools today and many of his phrases are used in everyday language.

3. Abraham Pineo Gesner (1797-1864)

A Canadian geologist and doctor who invented kerosene, a liquid fuel that was originally used in lamps. Today, over 1 billion barrels of kerosene are used worldwide every day for cooking, heating and in jet fuel for aeroplanes.

4. Guglielmo Marconi (1874-1937)

An Italian inventor, engineer, physicist and winner of the 1909 Nobel Prize for Physics. Marconi is best known for inventing the wireless telegraph, which paved the way for all modern radio

5. Mahatma Gandhi (1869-1948)

The leader of the nationalism movement in India, who used non-violent protest to bring about independence from British rule from 1858 to 1947. Gandhi inspired civil rights movements around the world and is often called the 'Father of India'.

6. Joseph Stalin (1879-1953)

A Russian dictator who ruled over the Soviet Union for quarter of a century using a regime of terror. Stalin helped defeat the Nazis and turned the Soviet Union into an industrial country. However, he also caused the deaths of tens of millions of his own people.

7. Edmund Hillary (1919-2008)

A New Zealand explorer who became the first man to climb Mount Everest, the highest mountain in the world. He later created the Himalayan Trust to build schools, hospitals and airfields for the Nepalese people.

9. Tim Berners-Lee (1955-)

A British computer scientist who invented the World Wide Web. He also developed the world's first web browser and website, which explains the World Wide Web: http://info.cern.ch

8. Rosalind Franklin (1920-1958)

A British chemist who helped discover the structure of deoxyribonucleic acid (DNA), the building block of life in all living things. Franklin's contribution to the discovery was not recognised until after her death at 37 years old.

10. Mark Zuckerberg (1984-)

An American internet entrepreneur who co-founded the social networking website Facebook. The website helped usher in a new era of online social media. Zuckerberg was named one of the wealthiest and most influential people in the world in 2010 by *Time* magazine.

TIMELINE

334 BCE
Alexander the Great lands in Asia Minor and begins his overthrow of the Persian Empire.

476 CE
Roman Emperor Romulus Augustus is deposed by Germanic chieftain Odoacer, marking the beginning of the end of the Western Roman Empire.

1066
Anglo-Saxon King Harold II is defeated by Duke William II of Normandy at the Battle of Hastings, which results in the Norman conquest of England.

1914
Austrian archduke Franz Ferdinand is assassinated in Sarajevo, leading to the outbreak of the First World War in Europe.

1903
Marie Curie is awarded the Nobel prize for Physics, making her the first woman to win the prize.

1865
The American Civil War between the northern and southern states ends, resulting in the abolition of slavery in the United States.

1917
The Bolsheviks lead an armed uprising in Petrograd as part of the Russian Revolution that deposes the Tsar and establishes communist rule.

1939
German Chancellor Adolf Hitler orders the invasion of Poland, marking the start of the Second World War.

2001
Islamic terrorist group al-Qaeda, led by Osama bin Laden, hijack four planes in an attack on the Unites States of America that includes the destruction of the New York World Trade Center.

1990
Civil rights leader Nelson Mandela is released from prison, resulting in the end of South Africa's apartheid system.

1969
American astronaut Neil Armstrong becomes the first human to set foot on the moon, signalling the end of the Space Race between the Soviet Union and the United States.

1215
The Feudal Barons of England sign the Magna Carter with King John, limiting the king's powers and setting out a new law of the land.

1492
Christopher Columbus lands in the Bahamas and begins his discovery of the Americas for Spain.

1633
Galileo Galilei is sentenced to life imprisonment by the Catholic Church for supporting Copernicus' theory that the earth is not at the centre of the universe.

1854
Florence Nightingale leads a team of nurses to aid British soldiers wounded in the Crimean War, where she becomes known as 'The Lady with the Lamp.'

1766
Thirteen American colonies sign the Declaration of Independence which proclaims they are no longer part of the British Empire, but instead a new 'United States of America'.

1940
Alan Turing's 'bombe' device cracks the Nazi code-making Enigma machine, enabling the Allies to understand secret German war messages.

1945
The United States drops an atomic bomb on the Japanese city of Hiroshima, leading to the country's surrender and the final end of the Second World War.

1989
The Berlin Wall separating western Germany from the socialist German Democratic Republic in the east is torn down, resulting in German reunification.

1955
Rosa Parks becomes a famous civil rights activist when she refuses to give up her seat in the 'black people's' section of a public bus to a white man.

GLOSSARY

abolish To formally put an end to something.

Age of Discovery A period between the fifteenth and seventeenth centuries when Europeans began exploring the world for goods, trade routes and land.

AIDS A disease caused by a virus.

Allies The countries, including France and Britain, that were allies during the first and second world wars.

Apartheid The former political system in South Africa in which only white people had full political rights and other people, especially black people, were forced to live in separate areas and use their own schools, hospitals etc.

artificial intelligence Computers and machines behaving with human-like intelligence.

assassinate To murder an important person, especially for political reasons.

atom The smallest unit of matter.

barbarian A member of a people not belonging to one of the great civilisations.

boycott The refusal to use or buy goods from someone as a form of protest.

civil rights movement The national effort made by black people and their supporters in the 1950s and 1960s to eliminate segregation and gain equal rights.

colonise Sending settlers to a new place and taking control of it.

conquest To take control of a place or people.

contradict To say the opposite of a statement made by someone else.

Crimean War A 1853–1856 conflict fought between Russia and an alliance of Britain, France, the Ottoman Empire and Sardinia.

decipher To understand and convert a coded message into normal language.

democracy A system of government by which members elect representatives.

depose To remove forcibly.

discriminate To treat a person, or group of people, differently from the rest.

enslave To make someone into a slave, who works for their master without being paid.

execute To kill somebody, especially as a punishment for breaking the law.

exterminate To destroy something completely.

fascism An extreme system of government led by a dictator.

heresy A belief or idea that contradicts the teaching of the Church.

hijack To illegally seize control of a vehicle.

HIV A virus that damages the immune system (the body's defences against disease) so that the sufferer catches diseases easily. If no treatment is given, the HIV infection causes AIDS.

Holocaust The mass murder of Jews and other people by Nazis during the Second World War.

Industrial Revolution The fast development

of Industry that began in Britain in the late eighteenth century.

invade When an army from one country enters another country by force to take control of it.

Islam A world religion. Followers of Islam are called Muslims.

leukaemia A life-threatening disease caused by an increase in human white blood cells.

liberate To provide freedom.

Milky Way The galaxy that contains our Solar System.

Nobel Prize An annual award given for scientific or cultural advances.

posthumous Given after a person's death.

prejudice A preconceived opinion that is not based on reason or actual experience.

regime A system of government, often one that is extreme.

Renaissance The revival of classic art and literature in the fourteenth to sixteenth centuries.

reunification When something is put it back together.

revolutionary To cause a dramatic change in something, such as a long-held belief.

Russian Revolution A series of revolutions in the Russian Empire during 1917.

sanitation Keeping a place clean from dirt, disease and infection by removing waste and providing clean water.

segregation The enforced separation of a race, class, or ethnic group.

smallpox A disease caused by a virus that causes fever and postules that eventually scar.

territory An area of land under a ruler or state.

treason The act of betraying your country.

unconstitutional Something that is not in agreement with political rules of the time.

uprising An act of rebellion.

viceroy A ruler exercising authority in a colony on behalf of a king or queen.

FURTHER INFORMATION

Books

Inspirational Lives: Nelson Mandela,
Kay Barnham, Wayland (2014)

Black History Makers: Campaigners,
Debbie Foy, Wayland (2014)

Who's Who in Science and Technology,
Bob Fawke, Wayland (2014)

Websites

100 historical people who changed the world:
www.biographyonline.net/people/people-who-changed-world.html

Time *magazine's most 100 influential people:*
http://content.time.com/time/specials/packages/0,28757,2020772,00.html

Famous historical people from around the world:
www.kidinfo.com/american_history/famous_historical_people.htm

Places to visit

The Florence Nightingale Museum: 2 Lambeth Palace Road, London SE1 7EW

Bletchley Park: Sherwood Drive, Bletchley, Milton Keynes, MK3 6EB

Imperial War Museum North: the Quays, Trafford Wharf Road, Manchester, M17 1TZ

INDEX

DISCOVER MORE ABOUT WHO AND WHAT HAS CHANGED THE COURSE OF HUMAN HISTORY!

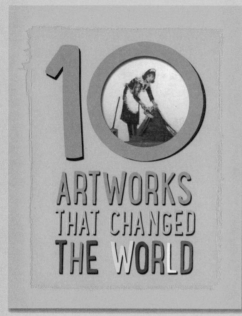

9780750291361

9780750291279

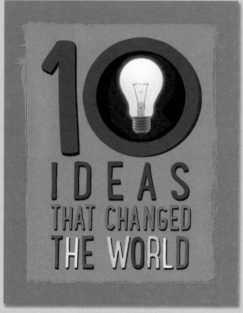

9780750291392

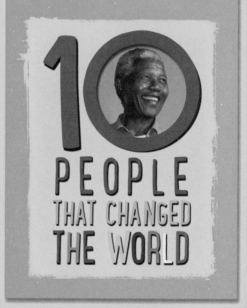

9780750291293

WAYLAND

www.waylandbooks.co.uk

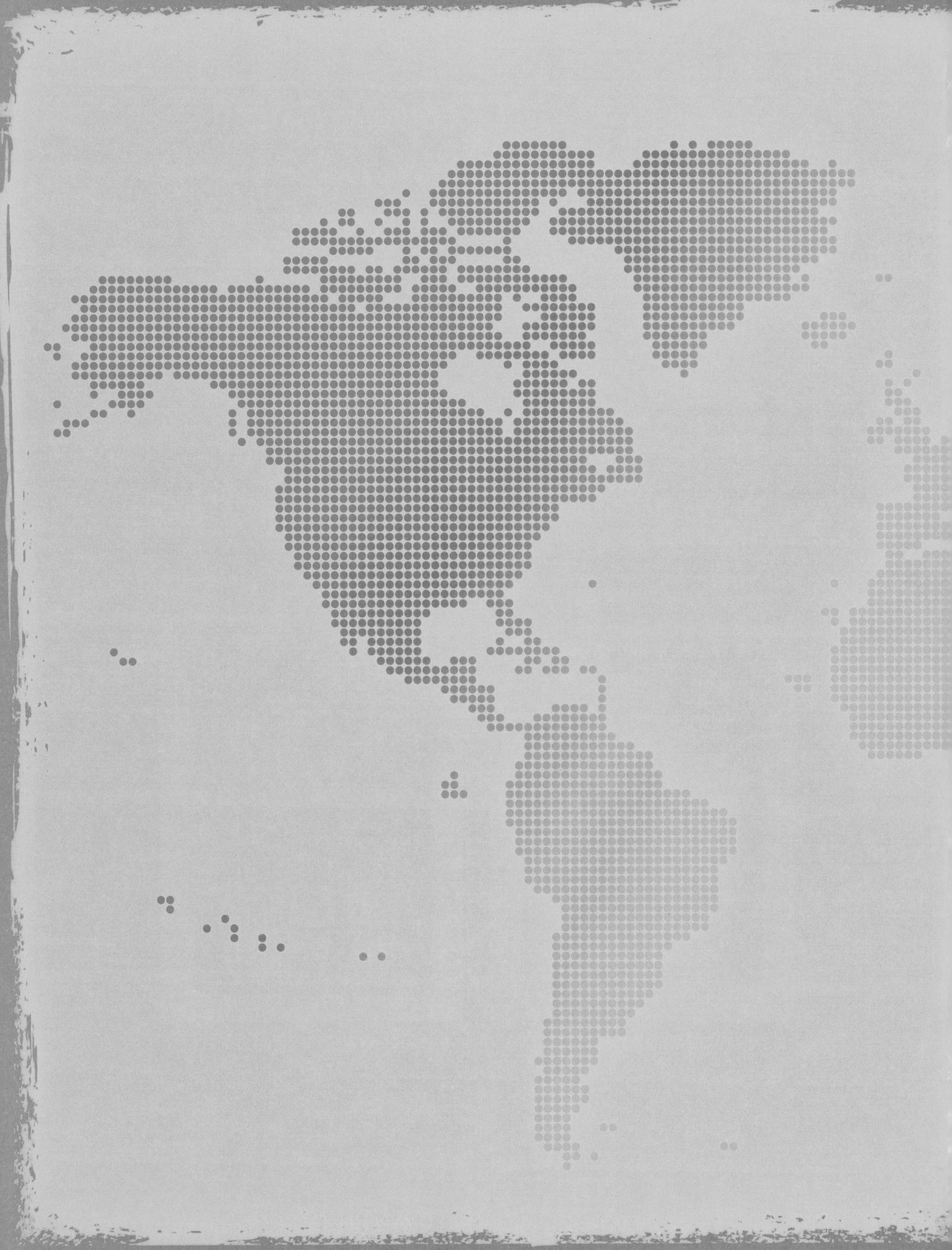